PASSWC

123456

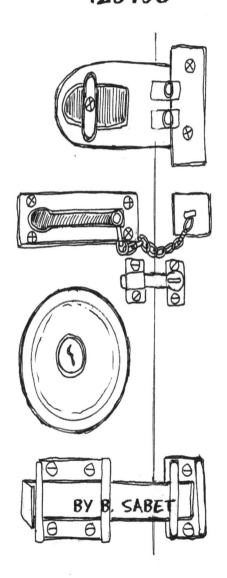

BY B. SABET

Name	
Website	
Login/user name	
Password/pin	
Security Question	
Notes:	

Name	
Website	
Login/user name	
Password/pin	
Security Question	
notes:	

Name	
Website	
Login/user name	
Password/pin	
Security Question	
notes:	

Name	
Website	
Login/user name	
Password/pin	
Security Question	
notes:	

Name	
Website	
Login/user name	
Password/pin	
Security Question	
Notes:	

Name	
Website	
Login/user name	
Password/pin	
Security Question	
notes:	

Name	
Website	
Login/user name	
Password/pin	
Security Question	
notes:	

Name	
Website	
Login/user name	
Password/pin	
Security Question	
notes:	

Name	
Website	
Login/user name	
Password/pin	
Security Question	
Notes:	

Name	
Website	
Login/user name	
Password/pin	
Security Question	
notes:	

Name	
Website	
Login/user name	
Password/pin	
Security Question	
notes:	

Name	
Website	
Login/user name	
Password/pin	
Security Question	
notes:	

Name	
Website	
Login/user name	
Password/pin	
Security Question	
Notes:	

Name	
Website	
Login/user name	
Password/pin	
Security Question	
notes:	

Name	
Website	
Login/user name	
Password/pin	
Security Question	
notes:	

Name	
Website	
Login/user name	
Password/pin	
Security Question	
notes:	

Name	
Website	
Login/user name	
Password/pin	
Security Question	
notes:	

Name	
Website	
Login/user name	
Password/pin	
Security Question	
notes:	

Name	
Website	
Login/user name	
Password/pin	
Security Question	
notes:	

Name	
Website	
Login/user name	
Password/pin	
Security Question	
notes:	

Name	
Website	
Login/user name	
Password/pin	
Security Question	
notes:	

Name	
Website	
Login/user name	
Password/pin	
Security Question	
notes:	

Name	
Website	
Login/user name	
Password/pin	
Security Question	
notes:	

Name	
Website	
Login/user name	
Password/pin	
Security Question	
notes:	

Name	
Website	
Login/user name	
Password/pin	
Security Question	
notes:	

Name	
Website	
Login/user name	
Password/pin	
Security Question	
notes:	

Name	
Website	
Login/user name	
Password/pin	
Security Question	
notes:	

Name	
Website	
Login/user name	
Password/pin	
Security Question	
notes:	

Name	
Website	
Login/user name	
Password/pin	
Security Question	
notes:	

Name	
Website	
Login/user name	
Password/pin	
Security Question	
notes:	

Name	
Website	
Login/user name	
Password/pin	
Security Question	
notes:	

Name	
Website	
Login/user name	
Password/pin	
Security Question	
notes:	

Name	
Website	
Login/user name	
Password/pin	
Security Question	
notes:	

Name	
Website	
Login/user name	
Password/pin	
Security Question	
notes:	

Name	
Website	
Login/user name	
Password/pin	
Security Question	
notes:	

Name	
Website	
Login/user name	
Password/pin	
Secuty Question	
notes:	

Name	
Website	
Login/user name	
Password/pin	
Security Question	
notes:	

Name	
Website	
Login/user name	
Password/pin	
Security Question	
notes:	

Name	
Website	
Login/user name	
Password/pin	
Security Question	
notes:	

Name	
Website	
Login/user name	
Password/pin	
Security Question	
notes:	

Name	
Website	
Login/user name	
Password/pin	
Security Question	
notes:	

Name	
Website	
Login/user name	
Password/pin	
Security Question	
notes:	

Name	
Website	
Login/user name	
Password/pin	
Security Question	
notes:	

Name	
Website	
Login/user name	
Password/pin	
Security Question	
notes:	

Name	
Website	
Login/user name	
Password/pin	
Security Question	
notes:	

Name	
Website	
Login/user name	
Password/pin	
Security Question	
notes:	

Name	
Website	
Login/user name	
Password/pin	
Security Question	
notes:	

Name	
Website	
Login/user name	
Password/pin	
Security Question	
notes:	

Name	
Website	
Login/user name	
Password/pin	
Security Question	
notes:	

Name	
Website	
Login/user name	
Password/pin	
Security Question	
notes:	

Name	
Website	
Login/user name	
Password/pin	
Security Question	
notes:	

Name	
Website	
Login/user name	
Password/pin	
Security Question	
notes:	

Name	
Website	
Login/user name	
Password/pin	
Security Question	
notes:	

Name	
Website	
Login/user name	
Password/pin	
Security Question	
notes:	

Name	
Website	
Login/user name	
Password/pin	
Security Question	
notes:	

Name	
Website	
Login/user name	
Password/pin	
Security Question	
notes:	

Name	
Website	
Login/user name	
Password/pin	
Security Question	
notes:	

Name	
Website	
Login/user name	
Password/pin	
Security Question	
notes:	

Name	
Website	
Login/user name	
Password/pin	
Security Question	
notes:	

Name	
Website	
Login/user name	
Password/pin	
Security Question	
notes:	

Name	
Website	
Login/user name	
Password/pin	
Security Question	
notes:	

Name	
Website	
Login/user name	
Password/pin	
Security Question	
notes:	

Name	
Website	
Login/user name	
Password/pin	
Security Question	
notes:	

Name	
Website	
Login/user name	
Password/pin	
Security Question	
notes:	

Name	
Website	
Login/user name	
Password/pin	
Security Question	
notes:	

Name	
Website	
Login/user name	
Password/pin	
Security Question	
notes:	

Name	
Website	
Login/user name	
Password/pin	
Security Question	
notes:	

Name	
Website	
Login/user name	
Password/pin	
Security Question	
notes:	

Name	
Website	
Login/user name	
Password/pin	
Security Question	
notes:	

Name	
Website	
Login/user name	
Password/pin	
Security Question	
notes:	

Name	
Website	
Login/user name	
Password/pin	
Security Question	
notes:	

Name	
Website	
Login/user name	
Password/pin	
Security Question	
notes:	

Name	
Website	
Login/user name	
Password/pin	
Security Question	
notes:	

Name	
Website	
Login/user name	
Password/pin	
Security Question	
notes:	

Name	
Website	
Login/user name	
Password/pin	
Security Question	
notes:	

Name	
Website	
Login/user name	
Password/pin	
SecurityQuestion	
notes:	

Name	
Website	
Login/user name	
Password/pin	
Security Question	
notes:	

Name	
Website	
Login/user name	
Password/pin	
Security Question	
notes:	

Name	
Website	
Login/user name	
Password/pin	
Security Question	
notes:	

Name	
Website	
Login/user name	
Password/pin	
Security Question	
notes:	

Name	
Website	
Login/user name	
Password/pin	
Security Question	
notes:	

Name	
Website	
Login/user name	
Password/pin	
Security Question	
notes:	

Name	
Website	
Login/user name	
Password/pin	
Security Question	
notes:	

Name	
Website	
Login/user name	
Password/pin	
Security Question	
notes:	

Name	
Website	
Login/user name	
Password/pin	
Security Question	
notes:	

Name	
Website	
Login/user name	
Password/pin	
Security Question	
notes:	

Name	
Website	
Login/user name	
Password/pin	
Security Question	
notes:	

Name	
Website	
Login/user name	
Password/pin	
Security Question	
notes:	

Name	
Website	
Login/user name	
Password/pin	
Security Question	
notes:	

Name	
Website	
Login/user name	
Password/pin	
Security Question	
notes:	

Name	
Website	
Login/user name	
Password/pin	
Security Question	
notes:	

Name	
Website	
Login/user name	
Password/pin	
Security Question	
notes:	

Name	
Website	
Login/user name	
Password/pin	
Security Question	
notes:	

Name	
Website	
Login/user name	
Password/pin	
Security Question	
notes:	

Name	
Website	
Login/user name	
Password/pin	
Security Question	
notes:	

Name	
Website	
Login/user name	
Password/pin	
Security Question	
notes:	

Name	
Website	
Login/user name	
Password/pin	
Security Question	
notes:	

Name	
Website	
Login/user name	
Password/pin	
Security Question	
notes:	

Name	
Website	
Login/user name	
Password/pin	
Security Question	
notes:	

Name	
Website	
Login/user name	
Password/pin	
Security Question	
notes:	

Name	
Website	
Login/user name	
Password/pin	
Security Question	
notes:	

Name	
Website	
Login/user name	
Password/pin	
Security Question	
notes:	

Name	
Website	
Login/user name	
Password/pin	
Security Question	
notes:	

Name	
Website	
Login/user name	
Password/pin	
Security Question	
notes:	

Name	
Website	
Login/user name	
Password/pin	
Security Question	
notes:	

Name	
Website	
Login/user name	
Password/pin	
Security Question	
notes:	

Name	
Website	
Login/user name	
Password/pin	
Security Question	
notes:	

Name	
Website	
Login/user name	
Password/pin	
Security Question	
notes:	

Name	
Website	
Login/user name	
Password/pin	
Security Question	
notes:	

Name	
Website	
Login/user name	
Password/pin	
Security Question	
notes:	

Name	
Website	
Login/user name	
Password/pin	
Security Question	
notes:	

Name	
Website	
Login/user name	
Password/pin	
Security Question	
notes:	

Name	
Website	
Login/user name	
Password/pin	
Security Question	
notes:	

Name	
Website	
Login/user name	
Password/pin	
Security Question	
notes:	

Name	
Website	
Login/user name	
Password/pin	
Security Question	
notes:	

Name	
Website	
Login/user name	
Password/pin	
Security Question	
notes:	

Name	
Website	
Login/user name	
Password/pin	
Security Question	
notes:	

Name	
Website	
Login/user name	
Password/pin	
Security Question	
notes:	

Name	
Website	
Login/user name	
Password/pin	
Security Question	
notes:	

Name	
Website	
Login/user name	
Password/pin	
Security Question	
notes:	

Name	
Website	
Login/user name	
Password/pin	
Security Question	
notes:	

Name	
Website	
Login/user name	
Password/pin	
Security Question	
notes:	

Name	
Website	
Login/user name	
Password/pin	
Security Question	
notes:	

Name	
Website	
Login/user name	
Password/pin	
Security Question	
notes:	

Name	
Website	
Login/user name	
Password/pin	
Security Question	
notes:	

Name	
Website	
Login/user name	
Password/pin	
Security Question	
notes:	

Name	
Website	
Login/user name	
Password/pin	
Security Question	
notes:	

Name	
Website	
Login/user name	
Password/pin	
Security Question	
notes:	

Name	
Website	
Login/user name	
Password/pin	
Security Question	
notes:	

Name	
Website	
Login/user name	
Password/pin	
Security Question	
notes:	

Name	
Website	
Login/user name	
Password/pin	
Security Question	
notes:	

Name	
Website	
Login/user name	
Password/pin	
Security Question	
notes:	

Name	
Website	
Login/user name	
Password/pin	
Security Question	
notes:	

Name	
Website	
Login/user name	
Password/pin	
Security Question	
notes:	

Name	
Website	
Login/user name	
Password/pin	
Security Question	
notes:	

Name	
Website	
Login/user name	
Password/pin	
Security Question	
notes:	

Name	
Website	
Login/user name	
Password/pin	
Security Question	
notes:	

Name	
Website	
Login/user name	
Password/pin	
Security Question	
notes:	

Name	
Website	
Login/user name	
Password/pin	
Security Question	
notes:	

Name	
Website	
Login/user name	
Password/pin	
Security Question	
notes:	

Name	
Website	
Login/user name	
Password/pin	
Security Question	
notes:	

Name	
Website	
Login/user name	
Password/pin	
Security Question	
notes:	

Name	
Website	
Login/user name	
Password/pin	
Security Question	
notes:	

Name	
Website	
Login/user name	
Password/pin	
Security Question	
notes:	

Name	
Website	
Login/user name	
Password/pin	
Security Question	
notes:	

Name	
Website	
Login/user name	
Password/pin	
Security Question	
notes:	

Name	
Website	
Login/user name	
Password/pin	
Security Question	
notes:	

Name	
Website	
Login/user name	
Password/pin	
Security Question	
notes:	

Name	
Website	
Login/user name	
Password/pin	
Security Question	
notes:	

Name	
Website	
Login/user name	
Password/pin	
Security Question	
notes:	

Name	
Website	
Login/user name	
Password/pin	
Security Question	
notes:	

Name	
Website	
Login/user name	
Password/pin	
Security Question	
notes:	

Name	
Website	
Login/user name	
Password/pin	
Security Question	
notes:	

Name	
Website	
Login/user name	
Password/pin	
Security Question	
notes:	

Name	
Website	
Login/user name	
Password/pin	
Security Question	
notes:	

Name	
Website	
Login/user name	
Password/pin	
Security Question	
notes:	

Name	
Website	
Login/user name	
Password/pin	
Security Question	
notes:	

Name	
Website	
Login/user name	
Password/pin	
Security Question	
notes:	

Name	
Website	
Login/user name	
Password/pin	
Security Question	
notes:	

Name	
Website	
Login/user name	
Password/pin	
Security Question	
notes:	

Name	
Website	
Login/user name	
Password/pin	
Security Question	
notes:	

Name	
Website	
Login/user name	
Password/pin	
Security Question	
notes:	

Name	
Website	
Login/user name	
Password/pin	
Security Question	
notes:	

Name	
Website	
Login/user name	
Password/pin	
Security Question	
notes:	

Name	
Website	
Login/user name	
Password/pin	
Security Question	
notes:	

Name	
Website	
Login/user name	
Password/pin	
Security Question	
notes:	

Name	
Website	
Login/user name	
Password/pin	
Security Question	
notes:	

Name	
Website	
Login/user name	
Password/pin	
Security Question	
notes:	

Name	
Website	
Login/user name	
Password/pin	
Security Question	
notes:	

Name	
Website	
Login/user name	
Password/pin	
Security Question	
notes:	

Name	
Website	
Login/user name	
Password/pin	
Security Question	
notes:	

Name	
Website	
Login/user name	
Password/pin	
Security Question	
notes:	

Name	
Website	
Login/user name	
Password/pin	
Security Question	
notes:	

Name	
Website	
Login/user name	
Password/pin	
Security Question	
notes:	

Name	
Website	
Login/user name	
Password/pin	
Security Question	
notes:	

Name	
Website	
Login/user name	
Password/pin	
Security Question	
notes:	

Name	
Website	
Login/user name	
Password/pin	
Security Question	
notes:	

Name	
Website	
Login/user name	
Password/pin	
Security Question	
notes:	

Name	
Website	
Login/user name	
Password/pin	
Security Question	
notes:	

Name	
Website	
Login/user name	
Password/pin	
Security Question	
notes:	

Name	
Website	
Login/user name	
Password/pin	
Security Question	
notes:	

Name	
Website	
Login/user name	
Password/pin	
Security Question	
notes:	

Name	
Website	
Login/user name	
Password/pin	
Security Question	
notes:	

Name	
Website	
Login/user name	
Password/pin	
Security Question	
notes:	

Name	
Website	
Login/user name	
Password/pin	
Security Question	
notes:	

Name	
Website	
Login/user name	
Password/pin	
Security Question	
notes:	

Name	
Website	
Login/user name	
Password/pin	
Security Question	
notes:	

Name	
Website	
Login/user name	
Password/pin	
Security Question	
notes:	

Name	
Website	
Login/user name	
Password/pin	
Security Question	
notes:	

Name	
Website	
Login/user name	
Password/pin	
Security Question	
notes:	

Name	
Website	
Login/user name	
Password/pin	
Security Question	
notes:	

Name	
Website	
Login/user name	
Password/pin	
Security Question	
notes:	

Name	
Website	
Login/user name	
Password/pin	
Security Question	
notes:	

Name	
Website	
Login/user name	
Password/pin	
Security Question	
notes:	

Name	
Website	
Login/user name	
Password/pin	
Security Question	
notes:	

Name	
Website	
Login/user name	
Password/pin	
Security Question	
notes:	

Name	
Website	
Login/user name	
Password/pin	
Security Question	
notes:	

Name	
Website	
Login/user name	
Password/pin	
Security Question	
notes:	

Name	
Website	
Login/user name	
Password/pin	
Security Question	
notes:	

Name	
Website	
Login/user name	
Password/pin	
Security Question	
notes:	

Name	
Website	
Login/user name	
Password/pin	
Security Question	
notes:	

Name	
Website	
Login/user name	
Password/pin	
Security Question	
notes:	

Name	
Website	
Login/user name	
Password/pin	
Security Question	
notes:	

Name	
Website	
Login/user name	
Password/pin	
Security Question	
notes:	

Name	
Website	
Login/user name	
Password/pin	
Security Question	
notes:	

Name	
Website	
Login/user name	
Password/pin	
Security Question	
notes:	

Name	
Website	
Login/user name	
Password/pin	
Security Question	
notes:	

Name	
Website	
Login/user name	
Password/pin	
Security Question	
notes:	

Name	
Website	
Login/user name	
Password/pin	
Security Question	
notes:	

Name	
Website	
Login/user name	
Password/pin	
Security Question	
notes:	

Name	
Website	
Login/user name	
Password/pin	
Security Question	
notes:	

Name	
Website	
Login/user name	
Password/pin	
Security Question	
notes:	

Name	
Website	
Login/user name	
Password/pin	
Security Question	
notes:	

Name	
Website	
Login/user name	
Password/pin	
Security Question	
notes:	

Name	
Website	
Login/user name	
Password/pin	
Security Question	
notes:	

Name	
Website	
Login/user name	
Password/pin	
Security Question	
notes:	

Name	
Website	
Login/user name	
Password/pin	
Security Question	
notes:	

Name	
Website	
Login/user name	
Password/pin	
Security Question	
notes:	

Name	
Website	
Login/user name	
Password/pin	
Security Question	
notes:	

Name	
Website	
Login/user name	
Password/pin	
Security Question	
notes:	

Name	
Website	
Login/user name	
Password/pin	
Security Question	
notes:	

Name	
Website	
Login/user name	
Password/pin	
Security Question	
notes:	

Name	
Website	
Login/user name	
Password/pin	
Security Question	
notes:	

Name	
Website	
Login/user name	
Password/pin	
Security Question	
notes:	

Name	
Website	
Login/user name	
Password/pin	
Security Question	
notes:	

Name	
Website	
Login/user name	
Password/pin	
Security Question	
notes:	

Name	
Website	
Login/user name	
Password/pin	
Security Question	
notes:	

Name	
Website	
Login/user name	
Password/pin	
Security Question	
notes:	

Name	
Website	
Login/user name	
Password/pin	
Security Question	
notes:	

Name	
Website	
Login/user name	
Password/pin	
Security Question	
notes:	

Name	
Website	
Login/user name	
Password/pin	
Security Question	
notes:	

Name	
Website	
Login/user name	
Password/pin	
Security Question	
notes:	

Name	
Website	
Login/user name	
Password/pin	
Security Question	
notes:	

Name	
Website	
Login/user name	
Password/pin	
Security Question	
notes:	

Name	
Website	
Login/user name	
Password/pin	
Security Question	
notes:	

Name	
Website	
Login/user name	
Password/pin	
Security Question	
notes:	

Name	
Website	
Login/user name	
Password/pin	
Security Question	
notes:	

Name	
Website	
Login/user name	
Password/pin	
Security Question	
notes:	

Name	
Website	
Login/user name	
Password/pin	
Security Question	
notes:	

Name	
Website	
Login/user name	
Password/pin	
Security Question	
notes:	

Name	
Website	
Login/user name	
Password/pin	
Security Question	
notes:	

Name	
Website	
Login/user name	
Password/pin	
Security Question	
notes:	

Name	
Website	
Login/user name	
Password/pin	
Security Question	
notes:	

Name	
Website	
Login/user name	
Password/pin	
Security Question	
notes:	

Name	
Website	
Login/user name	
Password/pin	
Security Question	
notes:	

Name	
Website	
Login/user name	
Password/pin	
Security Question	
notes:	

Name	
Website	
Login/user name	
Password/pin	
Security Question	
notes:	

Name	
Website	
Login/user name	
Password/pin	
Security Question	
notes:	

Name	
Website	
Login/user name	
Password/pin	
Security Question	
notes:	

Name	
Website	
Login/user name	
Password/pin	
Security Question	
notes:	

Name	
Website	
Login/user name	
Password/pin	
Security Question	
notes:	

Name	
Website	
Login/user name	
Password/pin	
Security Question	
notes:	

Name	
Website	
Login/user name	
Password/pin	
Security Question	
notes:	

Name	
Website	
Login/user name	
Password/pin	
Security Question	
notes:	

Name	
Website	
Login/user name	
Password/pin	
Security Question	
notes:	

Name	
Website	
Login/user name	
Password/pin	
Security Question	
notes:	

Name	
Website	
Login/user name	
Password/pin	
Security Question	
notes:	

Name	
Website	
Login/user name	
Password/pin	
Security Question	
notes:	

Name	
Website	
Login/user name	
Password/pin	
Security Question	
notes:	

Name	
Website	
Login/user name	
Password/pin	
Security Question	
notes:	

Name	
Website	
Login/user name	
Password/pin	
Security Question	
notes:	

Name	
Website	
Login/user name	
Password/pin	
Security Question	
notes:	

Name	
Website	
Login/user name	
Password/pin	
Security Question	
notes:	

Name	
Website	
Login/user name	
Password/pin	
Security Question	
notes:	

Name	
Website	
Login/user name	
Password/pin	
Security Question	
notes:	

Name	
Website	
Login/user name	
Password/pin	
Security Question	
notes:	

Name	
Website	
Login/user name	
Password/pin	
Security Question	
notes:	

Name	
Website	
Login/user name	
Password/pin	
Security Question	
notes:	

Name	
Website	
Login/user name	
Password/pin	
Security Question	
notes:	

Name	
Website	
Login/user name	
Password/pin	
Security Question	
notes:	

Name	
Website	
Login/user name	
Password/pin	
Security Question	
notes:	

Name	
Website	
Login/user name	
Password/pin	
Security Question	
notes:	

Name	
Website	
Login/user name	
Password/pin	
Security Question	
notes:	

Name	
Website	
Login/user name	
Password/pin	
Security Question	
notes:	

Name	
Website	
Login/user name	
Password/pin	
Security Question	
notes:	

Name	
Website	
Login/user name	
Password/pin	
Security Question	
notes:	

Name	
Website	
Login/user name	
Password/pin	
Security Question	
notes:	

Name	
Website	
Login/user name	
Password/pin	
Security Question	
notes:	

Name	
Website	
Login/user name	
Password/pin	
Security Question	
notes:	

Name	
Website	
Login/user name	
Password/pin	
Security Question	
notes:	

Name	
Website	
Login/user name	
Password/pin	
Security Question	
notes:	

Name	
Website	
Login/user name	
Password/pin	
Security Question	
notes:	

Name	
Website	
Login/user name	
Password/pin	
Security Question	
notes:	

Name	
Website	
Login/user name	
Password/pin	
Security Question	
notes:	

Name	
Website	
Login/user name	
Password/pin	
Security Question	
notes:	

Name	
Website	
Login/user name	
Password/pin	
Security Question	
notes:	

Name	
Website	
Login/user name	
Password/pin	
Security Question	
notes:	

Name	
Website	
Login/user name	
Password/pin	
Security Question	
notes:	

Name	
Website	
Login/user name	
Password/pin	
Security Question	
notes:	

Name	
Website	
Login/user name	
Password/pin	
Security Question	
notes:	

Name	
Website	
Login/user name	
Password/pin	
Security Question	
notes:	

Name	
Website	
Login/user name	
Password/pin	
Security Question	
notes:	

Name	
Website	
Login/user name	
Password/pin	
Security Question	
notes:	

Name	
Website	
Login/user name	
Password/pin	
Security Question	
notes:	

Name	
Website	
Login/user name	
Password/pin	
Security Question	
notes:	

Name	
Website	
Login/user name	
Password/pin	
Security Question	
notes:	

Name	
Website	
Login/user name	
Password/pin	
Security Question	
notes:	

Name	
Website	
Login/user name	
Password/pin	
Security Question	
notes:	

Name	
Website	
Login/user name	
Password/pin	
Security Question	
notes:	

Name	
Website	
Login/user name	
Password/pin	
Security Question	
notes:	

Name	
Website	
Login/user name	
Password/pin	
Security Question	
notes:	

Name	
Website	
Login/user name	
Password/pin	
Security Question	
notes:	

Name	
Website	
Login/user name	
Password/pin	
Security Question	
notes:	

Name	
Website	
Login/user name	
Password/pin	
Security Question	
notes:	

Name	
Website	
Login/user name	
Password/pin	
Security Question	
notes:	

Name	
Website	
Login/user name	
Password/pin	
Security Question	
notes:	

Name	
Website	
Login/user name	
Password/pin	
Security Question	
notes:	

Name	
Website	
Login/user name	
Password/pin	
Security Question	
notes:	

Name	
Website	
Login/user name	
Password/pin	
Security Question	
notes:	

Name	
Website	
Login/user name	
Password/pin	
Security Question	
notes:	

Name	
Website	
Login/user name	
Password/pin	
Security Question	
notes:	

Name	
Website	
Login/user name	
Password/pin	
Security Question	
notes:	

Name	
Website	
Login/user name	
Password/pin	
Security Question	
notes:	

Name	
Website	
Login/user name	
Password/pin	
Security Question	
notes:	

Name	
Website	
Login/user name	
Password/pin	
Security Question	
notes:	

Name	
Website	
Login/user name	
Password/pin	
Security Question	
notes:	

Name	
Website	
Login/user name	
Password/pin	
Security Question	
notes:	

Name	
Website	
Login/user name	
Password/pin	
Security Question	
notes:	

Name	
Website	
Login/user name	
Password/pin	
Security Question	
notes:	

Name	
Website	
Login/user name	
Password/pin	
Security Question	
notes:	

Name	
Website	
Login/user name	
Password/pin	
Security Question	
notes:	

Name	
Website	
Login/user name	
Password/pin	
Security Question	
notes:	

Name	
Website	
Login/user name	
Password/pin	
Security Question	
notes:	

Name	
Website	
Login/user name	
Password/pin	
Security Question	
notes:	

Name	
Website	
Login/user name	
Password/pin	
Security Question	
notes:	

Name	
Website	
Login/user name	
Password/pin	
Security Question	
notes:	

Name	
Website	
Login/user name	
Password/pin	
Security Question	
notes:	

Name	
Website	
Login/user name	
Password/pin	
Security Question	
notes:	

Name	
Website	
Login/user name	
Password/pin	
Security Question	
notes:	

Name	
Website	
Login/user name	
Password/pin	
Security Question	
notes:	

Name	
Website	
Login/user name	
Password/pin	
Security Question	
notes:	

Name	
Website	
Login/user name	
Password/pin	
Security Question	
notes:	

Name	
Website	
Login/user name	
Password/pin	
Security Question	
notes:	

Name	
Website	
Login/user name	
Password/pin	
Security Question	
notes:	

Name	
Website	
Login/user name	
Password/pin	
Security Question	
notes:	

Name	
Website	
Login/user name	
Password/pin	
Security Question	
notes:	

Name	
Website	
Login/user name	
Password/pin	
Security Question	
notes:	

Name	
Website	
Login/user name	
Password/pin	
Security Question	
notes:	

Name	
Website	
Login/user name	
Password/pin	
Security Question	
notes:	

Name	
Website	
Login/user name	
Password/pin	
Security Question	
notes:	

Name	
Website	
Login/user name	
Password/pin	
Security Question	
notes:	

Name	
Website	
Login/user name	
Password/pin	
Security Question	
notes:	

Name	
Website	
Login/user name	
Password/pin	
Security Question	
notes:	

Name	
Website	
Login/user name	
Password/pin	
Security Question	
notes:	

Name	
Website	
Login/user name	
Password/pin	
Security Question	
notes:	

Name	
Website	
Login/user name	
Password/pin	
Security Question	
notes:	

Name	
Website	
Login/user name	
Password/pin	
Security Question	
notes:	

Name	
Website	
Login/user name	
Password/pin	
Security Question	
notes:	

Name	
Website	
Login/user name	
Password/pin	
Security Question	
notes:	

Name	
Website	
Login/user name	
Password/pin	
Security Question	
notes:	

Name	
Website	
Login/user name	
Password/pin	
Security Question	
notes:	

Name	
Website	
Login/user name	
Password/pin	
Security Question	
notes:	

Name	
Website	
Login/user name	
Password/pin	
Security Question	
notes:	

Name	
Website	
Login/user name	
Password/pin	
Security Question	
notes:	

Name	
Website	
Login/user name	
Password/pin	
Security Question	
notes:	

Name	
Website	
Login/user name	
Password/pin	
Security Question	
notes:	

Name	
Website	
Login/user name	
Password/pin	
Security Question	
notes:	

Name	
Website	
Login/user name	
Password/pin	
Security Question	
notes:	

Name	
Website	
Login/user name	
Password/pin	
Security Question	
notes:	

Name	
Website	
Login/user name	
Password/pin	
Security Question	
notes:	

Name	
Website	
Login/user name	
Password/pin	
Security Question	
notes:	

Name	
Website	
Login/user name	
Password/pin	
Security Question	
notes:	

Name	
Website	
Login/user name	
Password/pin	
Security Question	
notes:	

Name	
Website	
Login/user name	
Password/pin	
Security Question	
notes:	

Name	
Website	
Login/user name	
Password/pin	
Security Question	
notes:	

Name	
Website	
Login/user name	
Password/pin	
Security Question	
notes:	

Name	
Website	
Login/user name	
Password/pin	
Security Question	
notes:	

Name	
Website	
Login/user name	
Password/pin	
Security Question	
notes:	

Name	
Website	
Login/user name	
Password/pin	
Security Question	
notes:	

Name	
Website	
Login/user name	
Password/pin	
Security Question	
notes:	

Name	
Website	
Login/user name	
Password/pin	
Security Question	
notes:	

Name	
Website	
Login/user name	
Password/pin	
Security Question	
notes:	

Name	
Website	
Login/user name	
Password/pin	
Security Question	
notes:	

Name	
Website	
Login/user name	
Password/pin	
Security Question	
notes:	

Name	
Website	
Login/user name	
Password/pin	
Security Question	
notes:	

Name	
Website	
Login/user name	
Password/pin	
Security Question	
notes:	

Name	
Website	
Login/user name	
Password/pin	
Security Question	
notes:	

Name	
Website	
Login/user name	
Password/pin	
Security Question	
notes:	

Name	
Website	
Login/user name	
Password/pin	
Security Question	
notes:	

Name	
Website	
Login/user name	
Password/pin	
Security Question	
notes:	

Name	
Website	
Login/user name	
Password/pin	
Security Question	
notes:	

Name	
Website	
Login/user name	
Password/pin	
Security Question	
notes:	

Name	
Website	
Login/user name	
Password/pin	
Security Question	
notes:	

Name	
Website	
Login/user name	
Password/pin	
Security Question	
notes:	

Name	
Website	
Login/user name	
Password/pin	
Security Question	
notes:	

Name	
Website	
Login/user name	
Password/pin	
Security Question	
notes:	

Name	
Website	
Login/user name	
Password/pin	
Security Question	
notes:	

Name	
Website	
Login/user name	
Password/pin	
Security Question	
notes:	

Name	
Website	
Login/user name	
Password/pin	
Security Question	
notes:	

Name	
Website	
Login/user name	
Password/pin	
Security Question	
notes:	

Name	
Website	
Login/user name	
Password/pin	
Security Question	
notes:	

Name	
Website	
Login/user name	
Password/pin	
Security Question	
notes:	

Name	
Website	
Login/user name	
Password/pin	
Security Question	
notes:	

Name	
Website	
Login/user name	
Password/pin	
Security Question	
notes:	

Name	
Website	
Login/user name	
Password/pin	
Security Question	
notes:	

Name	
Website	
Login/user name	
Password/pin	
Security Question	
notes:	

Name	
Website	
Login/user name	
Password/pin	
Security Question	
notes:	

Name	
Website	
Login/user name	
Password/pin	
Security Question	
notes:	

Name	
Website	
Login/user name	
Password/pin	
Security Question	
notes:	

Name	
Website	
Login/user name	
Password/pin	
Security Question	
notes:	

Name	
Website	
Login/user name	
Password/pin	
Security Question	
notes:	

Name	
Website	
Login/user name	
Password/pin	
Security Question	
notes:	

Name	
Website	
Login/user name	
Password/pin	
Security Question	
notes:	

Name	
Website	
Login/user name	
Password/pin	
Security Question	
notes:	

Name	
Website	
Login/user name	
Password/pin	
Security Question	
notes:	

Name	
Website	
Login/user name	
Password/pin	
Security Question	
notes:	

Name	
Website	
Login/user name	
Password/pin	
Security Question	
notes:	

Name	
Website	
Login/user name	
Password/pin	
Security Question	
notes:	

Name	
Website	
Login/user name	
Password/pin	
Security Question	
notes:	

Name	
Website	
Login/user name	
Password/pin	
Security Question	
notes:	

Name	
Website	
Login/user name	
Password/pin	
Security Question	
notes:	

Name	
Website	
Login/user name	
Password/pin	
Security Question	
notes:	

Name	
Website	
Login/user name	
Password/pin	
Security Question	
notes:	

Name	
Website	
Login/user name	
Password/pin	
Security Question	
notes:	

Name	
Website	
Login/user name	
Password/pin	
Security Question	
notes:	

Name	
Website	
Login/user name	
Password/pin	
Security Question	
notes:	